Rabbits

Julie Murray

Abdo
EVERYDAY ANIMALS
Kids

abdopublishing.com

Published by Abdo Kids, a division of ABDO, PO Box 398166, Minneapolis, Minnesota 55439.
Copyright © 2016 by Abdo Consulting Group, Inc. International copyrights reserved in all countries.
No part of this book may be reproduced in any form without written permission from the publisher.

Printed in the United States of America, North Mankato, Minnesota.

102015

012016

Photo Credits: iStock, Shutterstock

Production Contributors: Teddy Borth, Jennie Forsberg, Grace Hansen

Design Contributors: Candice Keimig, Dorothy Toth

Library of Congress Control Number: 2015941760

Cataloging-in-Publication Data

Murray, Julie.

 Rabbits / Julie Murray.

   p. cm. -- (Everyday animals)

ISBN 978-1-68080-116-3 (lib. bdg.)

Includes index.

1. Rabbits--Juvenile literature.   I. Title.

599.32--dc23

                    2015941760

Table of Contents

Rabbits

Rabbits have soft fur.

They can be brown or gray.

Some are white or black.

Rabbits have big ears.

They have fluffy tails.

Rabbits do not walk.

They hop!

Rabbits have long back legs.

They use them to hop.

Rabbits live in fields and forests. They live in deserts and cities, too.

Most rabbits dig tunnels.
Some build nests in
grassy areas.

Rabbits eat grass and clovers. They also like berries and tree bark.

Rabbits are fast. Some can run up to 20 mph (32 km/h)!

Have you seen a rabbit?

Features of a Rabbit

ears

legs and feet

fur

tail

Glossary

clover
a pea family plant that usually has small, round flowers and three-lobed leaves.

tunnel
a long hole in the ground dug by some animals to live in.

Index

abdokids.com

Use this code to log on to abdokids.com and access crafts, games, videos, and more!

Abdo Kids Code:
ERK1163